YOUR KNOWLEDGE HAS VALUE

AF140750

- We will publish your bachelor's and master's thesis, essays and papers

- Your own eBook and book - sold worldwide in all relevant shops

- Earn money with each sale

Upload your text at www.GRIN.com and publish for free

Bibliographic information published by the German National Library:

The German National Library lists this publication in the National Bibliography; detailed bibliographic data are available on the Internet at http://dnb.dnb.de .

Imprint:

Copyright © 1998 GRIN Verlag, Open Publishing GmbH
Print and binding: Books on Demand GmbH, Norderstedt Germany
ISBN: 9783668256644

This book at GRIN:

http://www.grin.com/en/e-book/335910/oscar-wilde-from-the-victorian-period-to-aestheticism-and-his-greatest

Angelika Felser

Oscar Wilde. From the Victorian Period to Aestheticism and his Greatest Plays

A Summary in Keywords for Preparing Oral Exams and Presentations

GRIN Publishing

GRIN - Your knowledge has value

Since its foundation in 1998, GRIN has specialized in publishing academic texts by students, college teachers and other academics as e-book and printed book. The website www.grin.com is an ideal platform for presenting term papers, final papers, scientific essays, dissertations and specialist books.

Visit us on the internet:

http://www.grin.com/

http://www.facebook.com/grincom

http://www.twitter.com/grin_com

Oscar Wilde

full name: Oscar Fingal O'Flahertie Wills Wilde

was born in Dublin in 1854

at the age of 20 he went to Oxford to study at Magdalen College

at Oxford he was deeply influenced by

Walter Pater and **John Ruskin** who were convinced of the fact that the full life was possible only through a devotion of art

John Ruskin: held that art should lead to a moral and spiritual elevation

Walter Pater: exercized a more significant + last influence on Wilde

in The Renaissance he found strange beauty in evil

urged that life should be lived as completely and fully as possible

in 1879 Wilde moved to London where he became a famous figure

here he was an apostle of the doctrine of **aetheticism** preaching to the Victorians (obsessed by duty) that the pusuit of joy and beauty was the chief purpose of life

a self-styled aethete in the characteristic attitude of the intense young man gazing at lilies or admiring the beauty of blue china

was caricatured in Punch, the British humour magazine-

received an invitation to go on a year-long lecture tour in the USA + Canada

giving lectures in the costume of the aethete Brunthorne (the poet in Gilbert´s and Sullivance´s opera Patience   - although poets such as Dante Gabrie Rosetti or Algernon Swinburne- both associated with the new aethetic movement- were more likely caricatured in it-) - in knee breeches, velvet jacket and a sunflower or a lily in his buttonhole

in 1884 married Constance Lloyd

in 1886 had his first known homosexual contact with Robert Cross

- later from 1891 with Lord Alfred Douglas-

the product of homosexuality was a series of **fairy tales** written between 1886 and 1889

The Happy Prince and other tales

criticism: 1889 The Decay of Lying

        1890 The Critic as Artist

his only novel   1890 The Picture of Dorian Gray

social commedy   1892 Lady Windermere´s fan

        1893 A woman of no importance

        1894 The importance of Being Earnest - staged in 1895

        1895 An ideal husband

1891 met Lord Alfred Douglass + formed an association with him

his father - the Marquess of Queensberry - started a campaign of scandal against Wilde

Wilde stated to take action against Q., however, at the trial, Wilde´s homosexual activities were exposed - resulat: Queensberry was acquitted + Wilde placed under arrest of 2 years imprisonment with hard labour

(De Profundis)

after his release, he assumed the name Sebastian Melmoth + left for Paris where he died 3 years later in 1900.

Most popular spokesman in the 19th century advocating the doctrine of aetheticism which insisted that

art should be concerned with art for art´s sake - not with politics, religion, science, bourgeois morality or other intentions

„all art is quite useless" - a view denying any Utilitarian function of art

Victorian period

beginning is dated in 1830 or alternatively

1832 (passage of the first reform Bill)

1837 accession of Queen Victoria

it ends with the death of Victoria in 1901.

Year 1870 is used to distinguish the early Victorian period from the late Victorian period

3

writing reflected contemporary social-economic-religious-intellectual issues such as

the industrial revolution + its effects on the economic and social structure (rapid urbanization, massive poverty- growing class tensions, feminist movement for equal status + rights)

the frequently derogatory connotations of the term „Victorian" in our times- sexual priggishness , narrow-mindedness- are indeed based on attitudes and values expressed by many members of V. middle class

poets: Robert Browning - Elizabeth Barret Browning [Sonnets from the Portuguese] - Mathew Arnold

essayists: John Ruskin [Modern Painters, ...]- Mathew Arnold - Walter Pater - collection of essays (Studies in the History of the Renaissance 1873)

novelists: Charles Dickens - Bronte sisters - Thomas Hardy- Wilkie Collins

within the Victorian era 2 literary movements are distinguished:

Pre-Raphaelites -   Aetheticism - Decadence

Pre-Raphaelites: in 1848 a group of artists including Dante Gabriel Rossetti William Holman Hunt organized „Pre-Raphaelite Brotherhood"; their aim: to replace the reigning style of painting by a return to the style of Italian painting before the time of Rafael (15th century) and the High Italian Renaissance;

ideals of these painters were taken over by a literary movement which included Rossetti, William Morris, Algernon Swinburne

Aetheticism

the aethetic movement was a phenomenon during the latter 19th century

movement stood in contrast to the prevailing thinking of society that any art had an aim, i.e. to teach moral values.

Criticises mannerism of Victorian society and can be considered to be a genuine search for beauty as an attempt to escape from reality

movement had its chief **headquarters in France**

The French writers developed the view that

art is self-sufficient and has no use or any moral aim outside its own being

the end of a work of art is to be beautiful (-its formal perfection).

The phrase characteristic of Aetheticism: l´art pour l´art - in English: art for art's sake

the **historical roots** of aetheticism are proposed by the German philosopher Immanuel Kant in his Critic of aethetic judgement (1790)

an aethete is to contemplate a work of art from a disinterested point of view says an object „pleases for its own sake" without reference to reality or the ends of utility or morality

in **France** Gautier´s Preface to Mademoiselle de Maupin (1835) is often quoted as one of the earliest examples of a new aethetic point of view; his ideas inspired Edgar Allen Poe and Baudelaire (who again is the leading representative of Symbolism)

views of French Aetheticism were introduced into Victorian England by Walter Pater (conclusion to Studies in the History of the Renaissance (1873) he pleads for love of art for its own sake) - Wilde calls it „he very flower of decadence" influenced (Swinbourne, later Lionel Johnson), Oscar Wilde.

Wilde: expresses these ideas in his essays → Decay of Lying (1889) and Critic as Artist (1890) which form the theoretic concept of his writing

The concept of a poem or a novel as an end in itself whose values are intrinsic (immanent) *has influenced the writings of* William Butler Yeats ( ), T. E. Hulme (advocated the hard, dry image" in his theories of imagism and who influenced Ezra Pound), T. S. Eliot (The waste Land - a central text of modernism)

aethetic point of view: art -instead of life - says life is a work of art

the outstanding example of the aethete´s withdrawel from life is Huysman´s A Rebours (1884) where the hero Des Esseintes seeks to create an entirely artificial life

Wilde´s flippant dictum:

„The first duty in life is to be as artificial as possible. What the second duty is no one has yet discovered"

Decadence

in the latter 19th century in France (Baudelaire - Les Fleurs du Mal) some proporents of the doctrines of aetheticism developed into a movement called „decadence"

This movement reached its height in the last two decades of the century -> **fin de siècle** (which connotes the prevailing ennui - Salomé: bored looks for sensation and sexual fulfillment)

the central idea of this movement was the view that

art is totally opposed to nature - in the sense of biological nature and

norms of morality + sexual behavior (Dorian, Salomé)

movement advocates sexual experimentations and a deliberate inversion of conventional, moral, social and artistic mores norms and mores

(Wilde, Aubrey Beardsley)

emphasizes

the artificial

the autonomy of art

need for sensationalism, melodrama

egocentricity - narcissistic cult of one´s self

the bizarre

superior outsider position of the artist vis-à-vis society

aethetic art: soul is pure <-> decadent art: soul is evil, derives pleasure from evil

dandy is the embodiment of aethetic ideal that one should be as artificial as possible.

Outward appearance important as regarded himself as a decorative artist whose material is his own body; Brummel: tried to please people with his person as artists try to please people with their works.

Wilde´s conception of Criticism in The Critic as Artist I

The essay was first published in the magazine The 19th century in 1890 under the title „The true function and value of criticism"(-> Mathew Arnold: The function of criticism at the present time, 1864) - when Wilde published his Intentions, he changed the title

form: dialogue between Gilbert (holds Wilde´s opinion) and Earnest (who takes the role of the advocatus diaboli) - essay = work of art as it provides many levels of interpretation

1) The critical faculty is superior to the creative faculty (<-> Arnold)

("It is much more difficult to talk about a thing than to do it")

2) creative faculty: has the tendency to *reproduce* things but the critical faculty means to *innovate* new

works of art

3) the critic becomes an artist himself as he transforms the work of art into a new work of art

➔ the work of art produced by the artist is only starting point or material for the critic

➔ the critic occupies the same relation to the work of art that he criticizes as the artist does to the visible world of form and colour

4) the function of the work of art of the artist is to inspire the creative fantasy of the critic

➔ critic does not want to see the object as in itself it really is (-> Arnold) but

on the contrary: to see the object as in itself it really is not!!!

His aim is therefore not the interpretation of the work but its *mystification* [„I live in terror of not being misunderstood, music is the perfect type of art as it never reveals its ultimate secret]

In the mystification the critic is able to put his own and *subjective* point of view (-> objectivity was claimed in the 19th century)

The true critic is therefore no longer fair, rational or sincere but „a temperament exquisitely susceptible to beauty and to the various impressions that beauty gives us"

Sincerity is absolutely fatal - the critic is only sincere as to his devotion to beauty + never he never lets himself be limited to any stereotyped way of looking at thinks.

True critic is always curious of new sensations - he has „the spirit of **disinterested** curiosity"

Wilde demands the **free play of the mind** as criticism is subjectivity or better: the record of one´s own soul.

New sense of seeing art - art is no longer connected with use - highest aim of art is beauty - „aethetics is higher than ethics (Moral)

a life spent according to aethetic attitudes is necessarily a contemplative life-(Pater)

Wilde : contemplation superior to action -> subtitle of Critic as Artist I: With some remarks upon the importance of doing nothing" [Lord Henry] - connected with form (,,form is everything").

The Relationship between Art and Nature in the <u>Decay of Lying</u>

Essay was published along with other essays (The critic as Artist ...) in <u>Intentions</u> in 1891.

Appeared thus at the height of the controversy over romanticism and realism in fiction.

Again essay is written in form of a dialogue - between Cyril (the older one but pupil) and Vivian -names of Wilde´s sons; by making the younger man teach the older man, Wilde shows that it is necessary to rethink one's own opinion and to be willing always to search for new aspects

main theme: relationship of Art and Nature

thesis: art is superior to nature and comes to the conclusion that nature follows art

   but: it is fortunate that nature is so imperfect as otherwise we would have no art at all

Vivian /Wilde states 4 doctrines which constitute the new aesthetics:

1) Art never expresses anything but itself

demands art for art's sake - the autonomy of art - art does not reflect the concerns of the age

this doctrine is to be regarded as a protest against realist tendencies which were to reflect contemporary social, economic, religious, moral issues; art does not reproduce its age!

Accuses contemporary writers (Robert Louis Stevenson Henry James) of being too truthful

Wilde: art is the only way to detach oneself from reality, from society's normal and moral system

2) All bad Art comes from returning to Life and Nature + elevating them into Ideals

he, on the contrary holds that life is part of art's raw material, which the critic recreates + transforms. He puts it into another form (form is the secret of life) - with beauty, he can establish the necessary critical distance towards reality as a beautiful object is always useless, disinterested

3) Life imitates Art much more than Art imitates life

external nature imitates art as our senses can perceive only those effects which we have already seen through poetry or in paintings we see fogs, sunsets and rainbows only because art has taught us to see them

-> Wilde highly ridicules the theories of realism

4) Lying, the telling of beautiful untrue things, is the proper aim of art

Lying is thus a medium to reject the general opinion following society's moral values

lying is the artist's imaginative power to keep distance from truth and reality

to be a liar the artist has to be frank, fearless, free, irresponsible, exaggerating, disinterested

is to see the object as in itself it really is not

the true liar's purpose is to live in dissonance with reality - with rigid forms

Salomé

a play written in French in **1891**

was translated into English by Lord Alfred Douglass, with illustrations by Aubrey Beardsley

Appeared in English in **1894** - first production with Sarah Bernhardt in Paris in **1896** when Wilde was in prison

in Britain is was not performed until **1931**

Wilde´s sources of inspiration were

> Gauthier´s Une nuit de Cléopatre

> Flaubert´s Hérodias

> Joris-Karl Huysman´s A Rebours

Wilde´s Salomé inspired Richard Strauss's opera Salomé (first performed in Dresden in 1905)

whereas Wilde shows in The Picture of Dorian Gray that human nature is grey, he draws in Salomé his blackest and most evil picture of human nature - wants to confront the pure Victorians with the evil within the human soul

based on an episode in the **Bible** where Salomé, daughter of Herodias, asks for and receives the head of John the Baptist

➔ her behaviour is ultimately evil as what can be more terrifying than requesting the head of a prophet?

Decadence here means particularly aetheticized violations of Victorian spiritual + moral ideologies

urban middle class assumed

> heterosexuality and monogamy as normative
>
> children and women as asexual
>
> women passive and were supposed to hold their husbands´sexual drives in check
>
> to a large extent sexual interest was removed from the bourgeois family and assigned to prostitutes
>
> sexual drives were to be held in check until marriage
>
> the restraint was not only valuable in itself but also a sign for careful management of one´s
>
> personal resouces - sexual potency was conceived of economically

Salomé is one of the few supremely decadent works of the 1890s

Wilde attempted to shock his audience by violating in a number of ways social rules of both the play's context and Wilde ' s current historical context -

wanted to step on the foot of middle-class values : "épater" le bourgeois (as Flaubert put it)

In contrast to Victorian women, Salomé is a strong woman who disobeys the Victorian dictum to control oneself - Salomé, however, says YES to everything - insists on seeing the imprisoned Jokanaan, dances for Herod only to reach her aim

Wilde shocks his audience by depicting Salomés lust for Jokanaan, particularly her bizarre final moments when she holds his severed head and kisses its lips -> regarded as morbid + repulsive

anti-Christian play

Wilde represents the religion of satan opposed to Christianity

Jokanaan, the prophet, represses his sexual nature, believes that the Antichrist will appear

Salomé, however, is a symbol of human nature - not grey but entirely black - she's cruel, lustful

one-act play - consists of an introduction and 3 major episodes which are marked by different moon phases

exposition: **moon is white**: appearance of Salomé

<u>central episode</u>: **moon is black** : encounter of Salomé and Jokanaan;

attracted by his white body (innocence, sterility), black hair (death), red mouth (blood, passion)

death of the young Syrian ; appearance of Herod + Herodias - episode moves towards

<u>conclusion:</u> **moon is red**: the dance of the 7 veils + the behading of Jokanaan + kisses J. and is killed

Wilde makes use of the symbolist device of the moon

as a unifying and recurring symbol to suggest the presence of mysterious forces associated with Salomé' s sexual perversity

Salomé cannot be dissociated from the moon

at the beginning, Salomé is a spotless virgin just as the moon is white - then she strips veil after veil off - in the end the moon turns red - might be a sign of her having yielded her virginity to Jokanaan

Salomé might be considered to be the „incarnation of Cybele, the pagan goddess symbolized by the moon, the moon turning red is a symbol of the aggressive, sexually perverse female whose sex impulse is directed towards the castration of the male

just as Cybele renders her virginity to Attis after which she tears out Atti´s sexual organs in revenge, Salomé destroys Jokanaan by beheading him - his lips as the object of her desire are cut off

Jokanaan (advocates Christianity) represses his physical desires, stands for Victorian ´s repression of sexual desires, evil

Salomé (advocates the cult of Cybele) lives the unhibited expression of her lust

Wilde: we should express the devil in ourselves instead of hiding it

-> as in <u>Picture o D G.</u> a point of balance between total excess and total renunciation must be found

The Picture of Dorian Gray

was published by Lippincott´s magazine in 1890 after which it was expanded in book form in the same year novel which deals with evil in human nature + the pursuit of evil beauty

Nassar: main characters are personifications of the art movement „decadence"

Dorian, as he degenerated becomes a perfect example of the decadent, his portrait, as it becomes

more and more evil, a perfect type of decadent art

preface: some kind of catechism of l´art pour l´art „all art is quite useless"

however, there is a moral in Dorian: all excess as well as all renunciation brings its punishment

Double Identity

Wilde criticizes Victorian moral values and hypocrisy - their rules were lacking ease so that many Victorians were forced to life a double life themselves

Dorian is forced to live a double life - torn between good and evil

his self is split into two personalities: a physical one which is his mask that he is wearing in society, a spiritual one

during lenghty periods of disappearance he lives his evil and sinful nature

is never discovered in his lifetime- would have meant his social ruin

the portrait mirrors both his narcissm and his moral degradation

only after portrait has been destroyed the split personality is unified

structure:

2 main parts: chapter 1-10, 12-20; chapter 11 of particular importance

1-3: exposition: main characters (Basil, Lord H., Dorian) are introduced

motif of portrait is presented, L. H.´s philosophical programme of Hedonism is exposed

4-10: meets Sybil Vane, falls in love with the actress, however when she acts badly, he leaves her: art has become superior to life and love

chapter 7 is climax (contains Sibyl´s suicide) and turning point (Dorian starts aetheticising evil- suicide is a marvellous experience for him, moral decline start, first changes in the portrait, hides it)

11: sums up 18 years of Dorian´s life - hedonist, decadent

12-14: murder of Basil + destroys dead body by means of nitric acid (Alan Campbell)

15 conversation

16-18 Dorian is persecuted by Sibyl´s brother James

19 conversation of Dorian + Lord Henry - they take stock - Dorian is tired of decadent life + decides to lead a better life in the future

20 stabs the portrait + in doing so he kills himself - portrait changes while he ages

Lord Henry Wotton

real protagonist of the action

highly corrupted man without scruples

introduces Dorian into the New Hedonism -

becoming a Hedonist , an artist, is a way to escape from time, decay, death, reality

„to become the spectator of one's own life is to escape the suffering of life"

he is an **artist** in the highest Wildean sense:

Basil: painting is a mere picture of reality, nature (Wilde: all bad art comes from returning to life...) for basil painting is best work but

Lord Henry: the critic: is superior to Basil, the artist; does not merely reproduce nature but innovates a new work of art (guides, dominates Dorian) - he transforms Basil´s work of art into a new work of art - which is even further away from reality - poisons Dorian's life by giving him the Yellow Book

Dorian

Basil paints him while he is still in a state of innocence

becomes the instrument of Lord Henry´s art

as in the Faust story he sells his soul to the devil - in exchange of eternal youth and beauty

Lord Henry makes him look at himself with new eyes - desires a division of art + nature -

as in Decayof Lying art becomes superior to nature

after Sybyl' s death his grey nature (good because he is influenced by Basil - bad because of Lord Henry's influence) *declines* : towards decadence his search for new sensations becomes less and less pure - is under the spell of the Yellow Book + finds pleasure in evil things

Lord Henry gives Dorian the **Yellow Book** (Decadence) - which poisons Dorian´s life

chapter 11:

Dorian has become just the hedonist (experiences for experiences sake) L. H. wanted him to be -

lives for the moment without regarding the consequences

full of egotism

hunger for pleasure, life, sensation- „Live be always searching for new sensations" once he has lived a sensation he needs another one

feels very soon the typical ennui of the fin de siècle

needs to detach himself from reality - devotes himself to perfume - music (Tannhäuser -opera by Richard Wagner and typical of decadents) - collects jewels + stories on jewels

after his murdering Basil, he finds himself unable to derive pleasure from evil things

Tries to escape from his life which he had dedicated to art and beauty - become a burden for him

he tries to destroy the painting and in doing so he kills himself

Basil Hallward

gives himself to life and corresponds to society's views but in his painting

„There is too much of myself in the thing" - has lost the abstract sense of beauty

is Dorian´s good angel or conscience

Sibyl Vane

she is childlike, pure and innocent when she meets Dorian

is the symbol of the innocence of the Victorians + her death might be interpreted as the decline of Victorianism vis-à -vis decadence

Wilde saw human nature in the 19th century plummeting from innocence into the awareness of the demon universe

she has to die because she gives herself to love and life rather than to art before she met Dorian, acting was the only reality of her life but Dorian brought her to something higher -something of which all art is but a reflexion

this is shocking to Dorian as he does not love Sibyl herself but the art forms she is able to create

Human Nature in   Lady Windermere´s Fan

written in 1892

his first theatrical success

society comedy dealing with woman with a past, a secret (A Woman of no importance, An ideal husband) [The importance of being ernest is a Farce]

belongs to the genre of   **comedy of manners:** English comedy of manners was early exemplified by Shakespeare´s Much ado about nothing, was given a high polish in Restauration comedy (1660-1700),

deals with the relations and intrigues of men and women living in a sophisticated upper-class society and relies for comic effect *on the wit and sparkle of the dialogue* - often in form of the repartee, a witty conversational give-and-take which constitutes a kind of verbal fencing match - and on the violations of social conventions and decorum for example by dandies. (William Congreve The way of the world), the comedy of manners lapsed in the early 19th century but was revived by Oscar Wilde or later by George Bernhard Shaw

Wilde´s wit and ironic humour aim at ridiculing the conventional morality of his characters

The main motif of the play is Mrs. Erlynne´s desire to re-enter society + to be accepted by it

The dialogue has the paradoxical, witty comments on society that made Wilde famous

is a joke on Victorian public

as in Picture, Wilde points out that human nature is grey, both good and bad

at the beginning main characters Lady Windermere and Mrs. Erlynne form opposites

Lady Windermere: Representative Puritan with a strict moral code (entirely good); cannot forgive people who have once sinned, allows no compromise, is serious [Wilde: seriousness has a negative implication as it is against creativity]

Mrs. Erlynne is regarded by society as completely bad (is Lady Windermere´s mother, abandoned her child when she was young and in love with another man who abandoned her in turn -blackmails Lord W.)

in the course of the action, both characters discover that their nature is grey

Wilde wanted to demonstrate that contemporaries are no longer innocent and pure - the entire age is a fallen one - Victorians are hypocrites - there is a clash between society and the individual and public and private life

Lady Windermere learns: „There is the same world for all of us, and good and evil, sin and innocence go through it hand in hand".

Lord Darlington: is the first **dandy** to appear in Wilde´s comedies

Wilde did not invent dandyism; he took over the dandiacal tradition by predecessors such as Brummel, Barbey d´Aurevilly: Barbey stresses the idea that the dandy is an individualist using his extreme wit to shock and revolt against the society he is forced to live in

Wilde´s dandies are aristocrats, whose elegance is a symbol of their superiority of spirit

they use their wit to shock society, enjoys breaking conventional values and points of view

Wilde´s dandies substitute ethics for aetheticism ,

are in search for new sensations and beauty - what counts for Wilde is formal perfection - the content is irrelevant

Lord D. sounds very often like Wilde himself: „I can resist everything except temptation"

Play consists of 4 acts:

I main characters are introduced: Lady Windermere (Puritan) , Lord Darlington (**Dandy**, attracted by

Lady Windermere, makes allusions to her husband being unfaithful), Lord Windermere asks his wife

to send an invitation for her birthday party to Mrs. Erlynne who wants to re-enter society- his wife

refuses but he has already sent the letter

II Mrs Erlynne comes to Lady Windermere´s birthday , makes acquaintances to society, is invited and invites people, is asked by Lord August to marry him, her re-integration seems to be possible;

Lady Windermere cannot stand seing Mrs. Erlynne and her husband together, she decides to leave him and to accept Lord Darlington´s proposal; she writes a letter to her husband which Mrs. Erlynne takes - wants to prevent her daughter from making the same mistake she did 20 years before - she quitted her husband and her child to run away with another man - became an outcast of society;

III Mrs. Erlynne meets Lady Windermere at Lord Darlington´s house - pleads her to return to her husband and not to make the same mistake she did - does not tell her who she is and what she has to do with Lord Windermere, suddenly the men arrive at Lord Darlington´s house - Lady W. hides behind a curtain - men discover her fan at Lord D´s - Mrs. Erlynne appears telling the men she took by chance Lady Windermere´s fan - the latter's honour is saved and she can escape from the place where she was hidden - men believe Mrs. Erlynne has a relationship to Lord Darlington

IV Mrs. Erlynne brings back the fan - Lady Windermere thanks her for having saved her from social ruin - as she tells her she couldn't bear loosing her ideals, Mrs. Erlynne does not reveal to her true identity - Happy end for the Windermeres´, Lord Augustus finally believes she has lost the fan while she was looking for him - she accepts his proposal- they will leave England to make a new start

The Importance of Being Earnest

written in 1895

belongs to the genre of **Farce**

farce is a type of comedy which is designed to provoke the audience to simple, <u>hearty laughter</u>

this play is a supreme example of farce, the <u>exaggerated character-types</u> find themselves in <u>ludicrous situations</u> in the course of an <u>complicated</u> and <u>improbable plot</u>

achieve their comic effects not by broad humour but by the brilliance and <u>wit</u> of the dialogue

plot itself is ridiculous (each young lady is determined to marry a young man called Earnest, both of them are furious when they find out that his name is not Earnest although he has pretended to be Earnest)

in the **dialogues** Wilde makes use of *misapplied logic* - a dialogue which sounds reasonable is actually nonsensical (Lady Bracknell)

name Earnest and adjective earnest (in the meaning of serious) are homonymous subtitle „A trivial comedy for serious people"- that is the serious Victorians

Double identity

Jack Worthing : in the country the respectable Jack Worthing

guardian of Cecily Cardew

this identity is only a mask, his true identity emerges when he goes to London

on pleasure trips- has therefore invented a wicked brother Earnest who serves as his pretext and excuse to disappear from social conformity

his real personality is the wicked one - but harmless

If Dorian had been exposed in his lifetime, he would have been rejected by society and disgraced forever - Jack is exposed but far from being disgraced, he is quickly forgiven by Gwendoleen

His double identity is a mere reduction to nonsense of the double life Dorian led, for it reduces his situation to the level of innocence.

Algernoon Moncrieff: in London: lives under the supervision of his aunt Lady Bracknell

has to behave properly and conform to social mores

has invented an invalid friend, Bunbury, who lives in the country

whenever he needs breaking out of conformity, he goes Bunburying

his revelation is not social ostracism [Ächtung] either but marriage (Cecile Cardew)

YOUR KNOWLEDGE HAS VALUE

- We will publish your bachelor's and
  master's thesis, essays and papers

- Your own eBook and book -
  sold worldwide in all relevant shops

- Earn money with each sale

Upload your text at www.GRIN.com
and publish for free